Between Rooms

Between Rooms

Poems by Mary Pacifico Curtis

Turning Point

Published by Turning Point

P.O. Box 541106

Cincinnati, OH 45254-1106

ISBN: 9781625491848

Poetry Editor: Kevin Walzer

Business Editor: Lori Jareo

Visit us on the web at www.turningpointbooks.com

To the bright lights
who inspired these poems—
Doug, Ashley, Julia and Michael

Acknowledgements

The following poems have been published, some ?
versions.

"Finally" (as "You Made Me A Slave to Silver") and
"Clousseau 'Clue' Curtis" were published in the *Boston Literary Magazine*.

"Between Rooms" was published in the *Naugatuck River Review*.

"Claritas" and "Cry Rain" were published in *Flywheel Magazine*.

"It Seems Not Long Ago" (formerly "The Face of the Moon") and "Surfaces" were published in *The Los Positas Literary Anthology* (2010 and 2012). "His Poem" and "Morning in Three Parts" appeared in the *2015 Las Positas Literary Anthology*.

"Special" was included in the anthology titled *Song of Los Gatos*.

"Defaced" was a 2012 finalist in *Cutthroat Magazine's* Jo Harjo Poetry Contest.

"Notes in the Key of See" was published in the *Minerva Rising* poetry blog.

Original art © Bette Linderman. Inspired by the author's text for use on the cover and in promotional materials with permission of the artist.

Contents

Cry Rain

slop on,
beat, drone
staccato drops,
rhythmic and random -
hit the roof, more
untuned brass
ensemble gone mad
together and not -
splash through,
flood gutters,
drains - spill
onto land
the place of change.

Morning in Three Parts

A twitch – pain – stillness
persistence - pricks - draws – pounding
scans - meds – weight loss - tubes
cameras – drains – wounds
consults in cold rooms - long
waits - white coats - handshakes, *we cans,*
bewildered hopefuls - harp reverberated lobbies –
wide stone staircases, whispery doors, an elevator glide,
another waiting room - translucent tangle of tubes -
tubes stuck between ribs.

Infusions. Drugs with x's and z's.
Weight loss. *Can't operate.* Infection.
Antibiotics. Waiting. Drains.
Pain. Weakening now.
Physical therapy, TPN, insulin, then
searching brown eyes meet their last morning.

Day in, year out, five years of mornings
I awaken in our bed, often thinking you here
finding the new pup who stares at me
with black wake-up-and-play eyes and the lab
who shoves her head into to my palm as soon
as my hand dangles off the mattress
I rub both dogs   roll myself upright
turn off the alarm   rush dogs over wood,
oriental rug and kitchen-cold stone to the door and out.
I could not be a pickpocket I repeat to myself, *because
my wrists snap - nor a cat burglar because my toes crack.*
As I think my silly thoughts I pass the girls rooms

empty now   and replay life as family in this house,
its refrigerator once stocked for four. Scratching
at the door tells me the lab wants in   the pup
will be next my morning begins
each day each year   opaque on this golden shore.

Surfaces

breeze wafts through vertical louvers
screened openings to outside - a slam
and my Basset's, "mmmmm-hmmm,"
his tail wags despite his diatribe against unknowns.

The redwood ceiling over my chair
holds the warmth of the man who handpicked
each of its boards, insisting on the most clear,
the most refined wood for this room
so we, and now I, can look up
with the satisfaction of seeing
the right choices, a job well-done.

I'm immersed in long red grain, even
from board to board, and crossbeam -
your ethic and care reflect in this room,
the one where I spend the most time now
and before you passed, the place
where you and I retreated.

Smooth leather of my chair
was the surface I sought
when lifting laptop to knee
to study your disease.

Smooth leather holds my ache of heart, ache of age
and new enterprise of living. At once cold, hard,
welcoming, the perfect
surface for now.

It Seems Not Long Ago

I carried my newborn in a pack
pressed against my chest. Her skin shone
milky iridescence interrupted by contours of almond
shaped eyes
covered by papery lids with hints of pastel, a round
face,
supple checks, wisps of blonde hair, shimmer of
eyebrows,
and that Cupid-bow mouth.
Her china-blue eyes
fixed their gaze on me until
some combination of motion and contentment lulled
her lids to close
and her head listed into my waiting hand. I could feel
her breath
if I put a finger near her nose, and sometimes her
puckered lips
sucked for a few seconds before relaxing to rest.
Cupping her head in my hand, I breathed in
imagining
that I held the moon —
perfect, silent and suspended til the break of day.

Twilight

our old dog sleeps, eyes half open
again the twilight of living

your eyes were wide
five years ago living

brown embers
meeting death

He has messages your caregiver said
as night fell over you, my love.

Defaced

inspired by The Rape by Renee Magritte

stars, glare, horizon
the darkening below bisected
by a milk and willow neck
upon which is a world

swirls in texture and mute
one pear eye one dimmed in shadow
nipple pupils
on a landscape without
cavern, cavity, passage way
for the intake of oxygen
the outflow of carbon dioxide, a call,
a spoken word, a scream, a song
a landscape without birdsong,
cricket chirp, wind rustle, a cry

a landscape of ordered flows,
up from, in many directions from
the blank and pointillistic shadow
a landscape of absence, bruised
of features, swollen emptiness
white empty, black empty
within the ordered flow
of going on, looking like
appearing, appearing well
well-coiffed, well-styled, well-preserved

well - healthy - appearing

pulled from shallows against the horizon
body - disembodied - face

within its frame and four corners
defaced again
embodied and escaping

His Poem

He brought it from Machupicchu   delivered with breathless narration
a treasure he wanted me to have   crushed in luggage,
tendered in pieces   intention in shards to be recovered.

More so than disposing of his clothes, the heartfelt puzzler now tempts me
requiring glue to set the pieces into satisfying assembly   the righting
of a whole   a vessel I now build matching corners into chipped corners
as egg shaped walls make layered story planes
a panel where mountain goats circle in cactus and grass
above, a flower angles to a hummingbird drawing out its nectar
atop the vessel, a cat arches with open mouth and fangs   an easy handle.

Cool in my hands now, this curious closed pot with stirrup spout
tells of long ago when felines held power for ancients
who shaped stone and clay effigy   artifacts buried
unearthed echoes through time   cupped in my hands
this pot   their voices and stories   his and ours whole again   mine.

Sixty Today
March 8, 2011

you would have been
(annoyed by it too)
if cancer had given you the chance
you would have been feisty
because you could be
you would have been
happy to have in view
green carpet foothills

> *you would chuckle as i redden*
> *what would you know of hot flashes*
> *you'd swear i look young and cute*
> *(you would too)*

you would have
dug through snow
last weekend at our mountain
cabin hideaway
counting on chocolate inside
and i would have it waiting

> *you would have walked outside with me*
> *to look at pinprick mysteries*
> *in their black universe*
> *we would have talked*
> *of UFO's and shooting stars*
> *that might grace our upward gaze*

i would have admired your profile
you would have wrapped long arms
around me
i'd feel that sixty could be ok

with you
if you would have been.

On the Strait of Juan de Fuca

3:28 pm
eyes closed

inhale exhale
repeat again

facing 70° east
4 inch herrings jump

so close to shore
salt

creosote of nearby debris
waves lap

children, fog horn, plane
uneven log rumbles sit bones

sun on feet
sand-burrowed toes

feather breeze
dry silk page

shells, claws, kelp, boys
the big one wishes
on a blue bikini

the young ones

pack grins and water guns

a diving loon breaks the surface
once and again.

Noetic

under morning fog
books break their light

I revel in parchment
reread, take notes and write

what, from shadow,
newly shines.

Kayaking

I haven't yet cast off from shore
skimmed the shine to sea
I haven't even left my chair
still rooted in this charge
of being a girl again,
with plans

packaged in the drive
through parched fields
round yellow hills
drying creeks
swampy spots
marshbirds
saltwater fliers
the push
to water
the curve
of Pacific Coast inlets
floating stringed buoys,
oyster beds.

I breathe in
friends
rippled crests, the sudden wave,
the wild possible
when I strike
into new time.

Leaving the Strait

You envisioned and tendered secrets I whispered
in poetry   made a safe place for my heart
we held each other between image and page
at the end you took me to a north-most shore

stepped off the pebbled concrete jetty
into wet sand   walked to the waters edge
stretched fingers to meet the lapping tide
flattened your hands into its foam

I memorialized the moment in a photo
you in a crouch   the foam   mist
shadow   mountains rising above low fog
unseen in the distance - an island of another country

you returned to my side and tho we both heard
the steady engine's drone you mentioned it
causing me to search the fog
for its source

finally I pointed   you saw too   a ghostly motor-craft
skimming through cloud and water
good thing radar works   I thought
to trust when you cannot see what's ahead

now we've returned to our places   our opposite coasts
we have what we have   a photo
the sound of that engine   the chilled twilight in mist

Enroute

waves reach and disappear

like hydrogen from the universe
circling close on the whim
of an elliptical spin

bones of ancient giants dusted
into daylight live and strike out,
shape and shame their extinction

the common ground is not

as pumping fists cry cacophonous causes
in sticky crowds, manifestos shift
borders, war chests, lives

matter

fine instrument of tectonics, a pendulum
sealed in arc between poles - ever in orb
the force of words that circle this celestial ball.

Clarity

I feel like I'm losing a good, good friend.
you're not losing a friend
you are dear

but of those middle-aged verbs
I'm interested in
we're marching along

i make my declaration
from near empty family home

mother no longer mothering
mate without a mate

asking myself if the blue flame rising
in me is instinct or the want of you

your painful corns
fear of the dentist
patterned nightly call

i reject them all
and tarnish of age
to strike out

traverse a coast
commune with spirit cultures
camp, canoe my misty lake

find clarity
unencumbered

Finally

I unpacked the finery and
found demitasses, glassware,
and pieces of china, the pastel
floral saucers you sent years ago,
forging a long distance bond
of shared sets and silver.

Four years after your death, I returned
to our early life as mother and daughter
through tarnish and compulsive
friction applied over the sink
with paste and my characteristic
determination to shine.

Between Rooms

The cold beneath my feet
once slab poured smooth, painted grey
to uniform perfection -

upon it we built a house
with a white kitchen, redwood-

river-rock-hearth family room,
formal living and dining
rooms off the foyer

I tell you this so you see what we built

a life with each other
with children and dog
cadences in connected driveways

I tell you this so you can feel

the cold under my feet, new foundation
of loss strangely pitted and stone
ragged with remnants of lives

I tell you this so you know with certainty

in the new kitchen cherry
and rift oak, vertical and
horizontal grains, raised ceiling

I have to grow taller to reach the upper cabinets

this concrete beneath my feet
is about to be smooth again - porcelain
butted against parquet

flowing into the family room
to hand-picked clear redwood -
I tell you this knowing I am opening too.

Becoming One

To Artist Tau Dong Dong

After redswell
of revolution
was history

and rendered smiles
went back to work

came the yawning baldheads
posed against dusty
sandscapes

elastic features testing
the limits of a face
and place

after many of those
and the ideas of many

there was one vision

water and light
the Buddha and the Virgin

flowed from camel hair bamboo brushes
to be sealed as one
with the dappled stream.

Chinese painter Tau Dong Dong depicts both Buddha and the Virgin Mary. He submerges each of their images beneath ripples equalizing them in a new continuum - the purity and the life force of water. To Tau Dong Dong this is essence after the landscapes and cynical realism paintings. He finds and applies brushstrokes to the flow of spirit.

For Julia

When you tell yourself your story
open with the universe -
evolution of stars
streaks of comets
asteroids that missed
moons hovering across horizons.

A sun blazing
at the center of its solar system,
its planets circling -
sing the third of those
slipped between clouds
above its land masses

its watery substance
it's great wall
closer

its trill mountain ranges
closer

its densities, city streets,
campuses, single buildings
the one where you are.

When you sing your story
banish dullards and nay sayers.

Let yourself rise tall
as oxygen surges

miles in molecules
through arteries to capillaries
fueling your words.

Tell and make it true.
Believe, my daughter,
as I believe in you.

Sail Away

Once earth and sky were mystery
linear time dappling water.

Then a wire-haired man formulated
proof of a big bang, black holes,

things he personally dis-believed,
little knowing that science would prove

his math
as pebbles prove water moves.

New math supposes we have the same conversation
at the same time in parallel universes,

raising the question of neutrinos traveling
near the speed of light, cracking time -

when no one can confirm neutrino speed,
when scientists disbelieve 'til proven,
when students simply wonder more.

What is the universe expanding into -

space stretching into the space it will inhabit,
or our bubble expanding into a larger container
that holds multiple bubble universes in which

two bubbles can collide?

Man cannot discover new oceans said Andre Gide
unless he has the courage to lose sight of the shore.

We sail away
the many of us in multiverse
lives to fathom.

Clouseau "Clue" Curtis

Lie at my feet, my boy, one more time,
fart if you must, lean and rest limbs
melt your liquid brown eyes into mine again
brush my leg with magic carpet ears
auburn peninsulas that hang to splayed paws
framing white fur with black and brown islands

Lumber your watered, slobbered, crusted
length for last strokes
rest here with me, with me
remember dusty hikes over parched boulders
muddy ruts and Sierra brush
where you, Buddy Boy, held forth
head and tail high,
happy to amble between your humans.

Lay your tumored torso here, just here with me,
stretch massive doggie digits before your next patrol,
baritone woo-woo-woo at full ring to echo and irk
new neighbors as your tail circles,
limbs loose again in pursuit along paths
and hillsides that heaven reserves
for beloved dogs.

Inspired by Uncle Isaac's New York abstract

He Returned From the War

and rendered the iconic park —
smudged between
loamy brown
shades of
paths, rocky rises
flats

and leafless cobalt branches
that weave and reach
veining umber buildings
whispered in the distance
on West 59th.   6th Avenue yawns
between the brick and stone.

There might be people
rushing through streets, the din
of horns, busses, and doormen's whistles,
jackhammers and the occasional
siren. But there is none of that
articulated within this frame -

merely structures rising finite
uncapped into a golden mist
contained by blue darkening above.
No gargoyles or penthouses
under decorated
roofs of the pre-war style,

merely a park in
the nation's largest city
smoky and ocher,
bathed in light,
empty of people.

Special
In the context of discovering a new super-planet

tucked at the base and nestling up foothills along the passage
to the western shore we are roughly thirty thousand
in the town named for cougars rarely seen,

we are conspicuous walkers of danes and shelties,
sheepdogs and yappy small dogs, retrievers, weimaraners
and the occasional pot-bellied pig

conspicuous consumers of marc, Michael, Kooba, Tory
and True Religion - it's said that
in the morning the German cars leave
to be replaced by pickup trucks with gardening tools
our traffic gridlocks when the high school
starts and ends its day

our town's houses once victorian, compact, historic
now sprawl across hillsides - mansions of competing splendor

our people have white teeth, glittering smiles, rich
colored hair, slim figures, high heels, butter leather
jackets and flats except

the few who camp by the creek —
tented or sheltered by plastic under the overpass
they whistle, mutter and bark - wear blankets
and holler into the gathering at our coffee roasting company
some folks kindly lower food to them
from the overpass sometimes

we coexist along the creek that connects mountain trails
to family park

share the soaring valley oak, coast live oak, coast redwood,
willow, sycamore and eucalyptus that domicile and conceal
mallard, blue heron, pied-billed grebe, egret, scrub jays,
redwing black birds, western pond turtles, bullfrogs
and Canadian geese that never fly north

share the soil taxonomically classified as a member of the fine-loamy
mixed mesic family of Typic Argixerolls - typically, brown light clay loam,
granular, slightly acid A1 horizons brown and yellowish red,
slightly and medium acid clay loam and gravelly clay loam Bt horizons
over sandstone bedrock at a depth of 36 inches - typical pedon Los Gatos
clay loam – annual grass and brush. (Colors are dry soil unless noted).

our Typic Argixerolls spreads on steep to very steep mountainous
areas at elevations of 200 to 400 feet - formed in residuum
from sandstone, shale and metasedimentary rock
under a climate that is subhumid mesothermal
warm dry summers, cool moist winters

mean annual precipitation of 20 to 70 inches
mean annual temperature of 52 to 56 degrees F
average January temperature of about 47 degrees F
average July temperature of about 68 degrees F
and a freeze free season of about 200 to 330 days

all of which means we warm ourselves in sunshine
under mostly azure skies look up at frothy whips and puffs of cloud
certainly not seeing the multiverse or even GJ 667C

newly found with ecosystem and proximity that hold the possibility
of life like ours, perhaps a town of people
perhaps as special as we.

25 Years After I Imagined You

for Ashley

fluttering life inside me

nested wings not ready for flight
fishbody shivers - you poked and pushed

my belly and my dreams

in a world full of other people's children.
our love's own lightening

our Buddha baby, our chickadee

common petunia and rarest rose
you've grown now

- your smile from the Challenger Deep

with grace to soar on comets' tails,
you tender even the smallest heart

in your luminous becoming.

Notes in the Key of See

Skat,
sticks, bongos,
congas, keys

alto
and soprano sax
one man sings - another

and another bows, blows and strums -
one cues the rest.
color-gelled,

their bobbing heads
liquid fingers
pumping feet

their caps, vests, violins
and big cellos
shiver and hum history

of island and rhythms
wind through fronds, brushstroke
tides, sizzling streets under cobbled heat

linen bands 'round virgin brims
sweat streaming on shades of brown
skin – stompin' spats, tobacco grins, fat ties,

closed eyes, heads bobbing, hips easy
to the five-eight bloodrush thrum -
of glories and defeats.

Chamber of Many Conversations

Dawn filters through clerestories
lighting wooden ladders that reach
from ground to archived voices,

and slide on rails from sighted eyes
that no longer see
to locked books that make
happiness into mystery.

They glide through fabled particles
suspended as the sun's
full glare floods in
to cushion edges of emptiness,

and glaze the hair
of a generation sprawled amidst
leathered hope and perfect-bound
expectation,

with volume sequenced questions,
and scrolls yet unrolled
- their script of dues
for life.

Secure panels whisper open
to dim-lit passages that echo epiphanies of the past,
as new lovers fade into shadows to trace
unfamiliar flesh, urgent

yet aching still for contours
of the ones now gone.
Twilight will turn to night
but not silence

in this din of hushed voices and vision

of days past that herald days to come,
the new story, the glow as sudden stars
renounce the dark.

You Reach For Me

and I for you - we step into our maiden orb
around this flimsy globe together
after other days and loves now gone

that smolder still when trembled
by the burst and pale
from coronet and lone sax bell.

Loves released on a breeze from sun warmed bluffs
now rest in rolling seas, and anchor darkest loam
under ebony skies' abundant embers of another time.

You and I danced once with death finding
only muted heavens and the crescent moon
- our mortal arcs between two waning sliver ends.

From black new skies we rose
and traced our hope for singular orbs
grounded in our waxing light. Then

with launching fire and hungry metal weight
we walked paces from the past
to rest beneath Orion's muscled glow

until ecru and goldenrod broke through
the nighttime skies
and corals crimsoned overhead.

I take you now as you take me
your music in my heart

my syllables, your syncopation
penumbra of our time.

Dear Ones

We have chosen this day to let you know
that together, we celebrate in March
and April, birthdays of much loved spouses
claimed by cancer.

We are aware
that we're not the only ones who lost
these dear and celebrated lights.
Family and friends have honored them,
made memorials in their names.

We know each of you
loved the person you lost as we hold
that person in our hearts
forever.

In our coming together as man and wife,
we forged new bonds with each of them
woven by sharing their artifacts
and histories into the fabric
of our love.

As they left us
both sent us
onward
to live happy lives,
to stay close to love.

We are blest with the riches
of days now done, the embrace
of our dear ones, and with finding
each other.

Together Now

soon Rainier is ghosted
in the northern sky
beyond the waterways
our road rolls south.

patterned pines
weave up tall slopes
and I know
with you I am where I have longed to go.

canyons between iconic peaks
evoke the seabed rising
and colliding with the continent
in ancient times,

and now, the staggered jag tapers
topward, erect in perfect pose,
they posture to the midday blue,
disorder in formation.

fallen vultures in final wingspan
dot shoulders of the road -
rolling foothills dwarf lambs grazing
to sheep size in sunset-soft grass.

under seaside stars, we stop
to open arms and hearts
before we sleep - and wake
as source and sustenance.

Mary Curtis writes poetry, memoir and literary criticism, and is an avid photographer. She is currently leading an eclectic life that combines working on a new collection of poetry and a chapbook of remembered stories, juggling business interests and travel to places that inspire wonder, discovery and more writing.

Devoting time to creative writing fulfills a dream following her career as founder and CEO of a leading Silicon Valley PR and strategic communications firm - for which she received the American Advertising Federation's Silver Medal Award recognizing industry excellence and social responsibility. She received her undergraduate degree from Northwestern University and MFA from Goddard College.

Mary has two grown daughters and lives on a terraced hillside with her husband, two dogs and sightings of wildlife that make appearances on a regular basis.

Thanks to those who launch poetry – the words when words fail, the smaller acts that appear in regions and journals that should be called 'heart'.

Thank you especially to Kevin Walzer and Lori Jareo.

61141762R00036

Made in the USA
Lexington, KY
01 March 2017